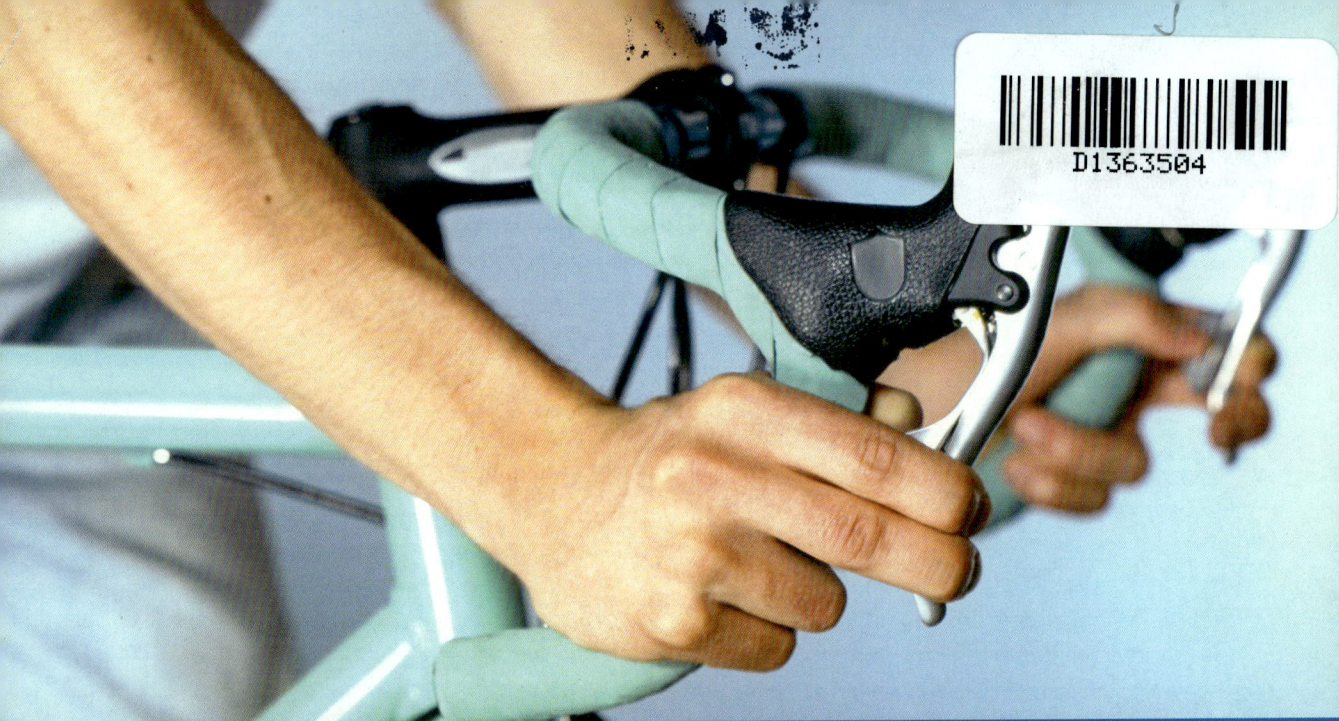

Contents

AV² Book Code	2
One Bike, Many Parts	4
Making Frame Tubes	6
At the Bicycle Factory	10
The Wheels	16
Gears and Chain	20
Handlebars, Brake Levers, and Gearshifts	22
The Seat	24
Testing the Bike	26
Your Bicycle	28
Quiz	30
Key Words/Index	31
Log on to www.av2books.com	32

One Bike, Many Parts

Do you know how to ride a bicycle? People ride bikes to work, for fun, or for exercise. Some people ride a bike instead of driving a car. Bikes come in many colors, shapes, and styles. Some are cruisers. They have high handlebars. Some are dirt bikes. They have thick tires and are good for trails. Some are made for speed. They are light so they can move fast.

Have you thought about how bicycles are made? There are many steps. Take a close look at a bicycle. How many different parts do you see? These parts are made at different places. Then, they are brought to a bicycle factory. They are put together on the frame. The frame holds all the bicycle parts together.

More than 105 million bikes are made every year around the world.

Riding a bicycle is both fun and great exercise. Bicycles allow people to move much faster than walking.

Bicycles

Different kinds of metals are mined from the ground to make a bicycle frame.

6   How Do They Make That?

Making Frame Tubes

The frame of a bicycle is the most important part. The other parts of the bike are put on the frame. A bike frame must be strong, but it must also be light. Most bike frames are made from metal tubes. The tubes are **welded** together. They are usually made from steel. Some are made from **titanium**, **aluminum**, or other metals.

Bicycles · 7

When metal is heated up to very high temperatures, it can be formed into different shapes.

8   How Do They Make That?

Metal must be mined, or dug from the ground. Steel is an **alloy**. It is made by mixing iron with **carbon** or other kinds of metals. At a steel factory, the iron is heated in a furnace. It becomes a liquid. Then, other metals are mixed with the iron. It is now liquid steel.

The liquid steel is poured into **molds** to form blocks. The blocks are then heated in a furnace. They are made into a round shape. Strong rollers shape the metal. Then, a machine makes the hole that goes through the center of the tube. All of this is done while the metal is very hot. The metal cools and becomes hard. Then, the tubes are sent to the bicycle factory.

At the Bicycle Factory

The tubes are all the same length when they arrive at the factory. A bike frame is made from different sizes of tubes. A special machine cuts the tubes. It makes the lengths that will be needed for the frame.

Next, the tubes are shaped by a machine. The tubes are fed through a series of rollers. The tubes may be made thinner in some places and thicker in others. They may be shaped into curves. It depends on the design of the bike. Another machine cuts the ends of the tubes. The tubes need to fit into each other when the frame is put together.

Rollers are used to bend and shape the tubes.

Bicycles 11

To make the frame, a machine welds the tubes together. This is done at very high temperatures. The **joints** get so hot that they glow bright orange. It takes about four minutes for the welds to cool down. This must be done several times to make the whole frame. Welding can make the frame crooked. A worker uses another machine to make the frame straight.

Next, the frame is painted. The paint makes the frame look good. It also helps to keep it from rusting. Some frames are painted by workers using spray guns. Other frames can be painted by moving through spraying machines.

Welding metal together creates sparks. Welders wear a face mask so they do not hurt their eyes or their face.

Bicycles 13

Unlike other paints, bike paint is not a liquid. It sprays out in a fine powder. Have you heard of **static electricity**? Static electricity is used to paint bike frames. Have you rubbed a balloon on your hair and stuck it to a wall? The bicycle paint sticks to the frame in the same way. **Electrons** in the frame and the paint pull on each other. The frames are baked for 15 minutes in an oven. This makes the paint hard and shiny. The frames then cool and workers add different stickers.

In other areas of the factory, workers build and add other bike parts. The frame moves to different workshops in the factory. At each workshop, new parts are added by workers with special tools. Screws, nuts, and bolts keep the different parts on the frame. The frame is placed upside down. The workers can reach the part of the frame that they need.

The frames can be sprayed with many different colors of paint.

Bicycles 15

Spokes make the wheel strong and keep it from being bent out of shape.

The Wheels

Wheels are important parts of a bike. A wheel has a rim and tire. The round edge of a wheel is called the rim. It is usually made from metal that has been rolled into a hoop shape. A machine drills holes all around the rim. These holes will hold the spokes.

Most bikes have 28, 32, or 36 spokes. The spokes are made from steel. Look at the wheel of a bike. Each spoke starts at the rim. It goes through a hole in the **hub** at the center of the wheel. The spoke ends at another place in the rim.

About 100,000 workers in the United States design, make, ship, or sell bicycles.

The rim holds the bicycle tire and inner tube.

18   How Do They Make That?

A worker puts the spokes in the rim. A machine screws the spokes into place. Another machine tightens the spokes. They all need to have the right **tension**. If the tension is wrong, the rims will be crooked. Another machine makes sure the wheel's sides are straight.

The last step is to put the rubber tire and the inner tube on. The stretchy tube is filled with air. Then, the wheel is done.

The back wheel is put onto the frame. The front wheel is put onto a piece of metal called the fork. The top of the fork runs through a metal tube in the frame. It connects to the handlebars. When you turn the handlebars, the front wheel also turns. This lets you steer the bike.

Have you ever had a flat bike tire? Something probably put a hole in the inner tube. This let the air out.

Gears and Chain

Workers put on the gears and chain. The gears and chain have an important job. When you pedal, you move the crank. The crank is a metal piece that connects to the gears. The gears connect to the chain. Together, they make the back wheel spin. This makes the whole bike move forward.

Bicycles have two sets of gears. The gears are the spiky metal discs that hold the chain. One set of gears is on the right side of the bicycle frame. The second set of gears connects to the hub of the back wheel. Different sizes of gears make the bike easier or harder to pedal. When the chain is on small gears, the bike is easier to pedal. Smaller gears are good for riding up hills.

The gears are connected by chains. They can create resistance when pedaling.

Bicycles 21

Some handlebars are wrapped with tape or fitted with rubber.

Handlebars, Brake Levers, and Gearshifts

Bike handlebars are made from bent metal tubes. The metal may be shaped in different ways. Some handlebars are straight and some are curved. This helps your hands grip the handlebars.

Workers put brake levers and gearshifts onto the handlebars. After the handlebars are on the bike, cables are run along the frame. They connect the brake levers to the brake pads. The brake pads are put above each of the wheels. When you squeeze the brake levers, it pulls the cable. The cable makes the brake pads push against the wheel rims. This slows down your bicycle.

The gearshifts also connect to cables on the bicycle frame. These cables connect to the gears. This switches the chain from one gear to another.

The Seat

What is inside the seat of your bicycle? The core of a bicycle seat is made from hard plastic. Plastic is heated until it turns into a thick liquid. Then, it is forced into a mold. The plastic cools and hardens. Then, it is taken out of the mold.

The next step is to glue foam padding to the plastic. A worker sprays glue over the plastic seat. Then, the worker presses the padding in place. The last step is to add the cover. The seat cover may be made from vinyl, leather, or rubber. It is cut to the right shape. A worker sprays glue to the seat. Then, the cover is wrapped around and under the seat. The cover is stapled to help keep it on.

A metal tube is put at the bottom of the seat. This is used to connect the seat to the frame. The seat is often put onto the bike at the store, not at the factory.

Bicycle seats can be adjusted for any height.

Bicycles 25

If something is not right, it is fixed before the bike is shipped.

Testing the Bike

With so many different parts, a lot can go wrong putting a bike together. This is why every bike is tested. Workers test the brakes and the gears to make sure each works smoothly. The frame and the wheels are checked.

When a bike passes its tests, it is put into a box for shipping. It may be stored in a warehouse. Many bikes are made around the world. They travel by cargo ship before being loaded into trains or trucks. They are then sent to stores.

Nearly 20 million bicycles are sold in the United States every year.

Your Bicycle

A bicycle arrives at the store and is put on display. You can buy a bicycle at a bike store, a sporting goods store, a large toy store, or a variety store. You can also buy a bike and put it together yourself.

It is important to take good care of your bike so that it will always work well and you will be safe. You should test your brakes to make sure they work every time you ride. Make sure to also check your tires to be certain they have enough air. If there is something wrong with your bike, do not ride it. Ask an adult to fix it or to bring it to a bicycle repair shop.

A bicycle is not only fun to ride, it is also a great way to get from one place to another. Remember to ride your bike safely. Wear a helmet and watch out for traffic. Then, choose a place to go.

People who work in bike stores can help you find the right bicycle.

Bicycles 29

Quiz

Match the steps with the pictures.

A. Metal melted

B. Tubes are bent

C. Frame welded

D. Wheels laced with spokes

E. Other parts added

F. To the store

1

2

3

4

5

6

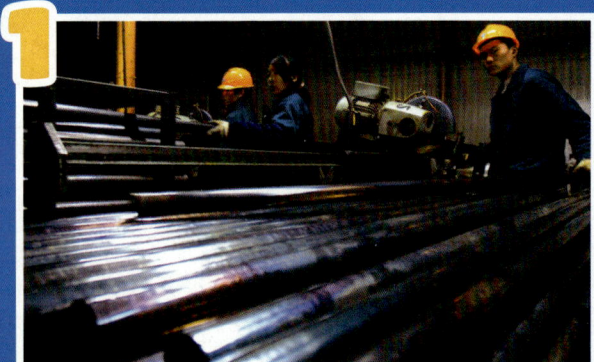

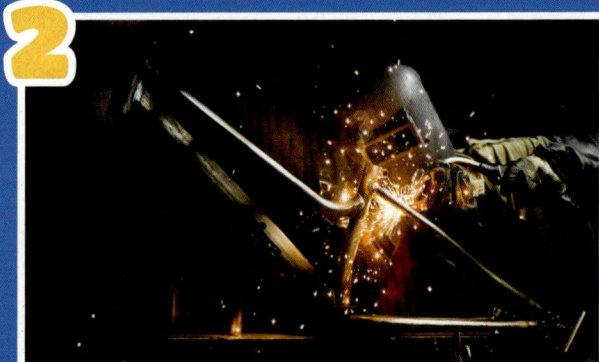

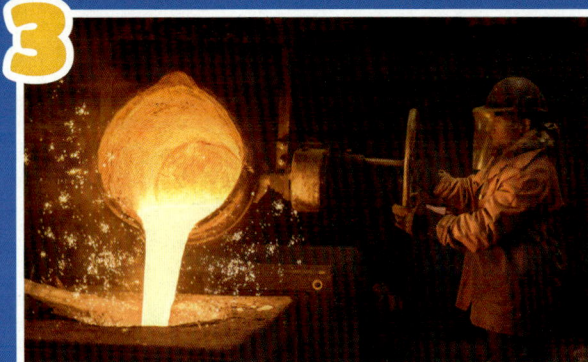

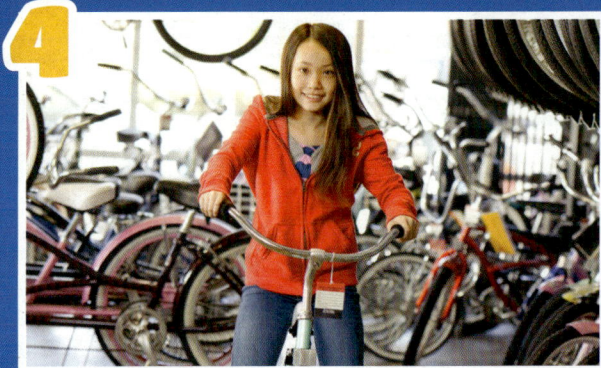

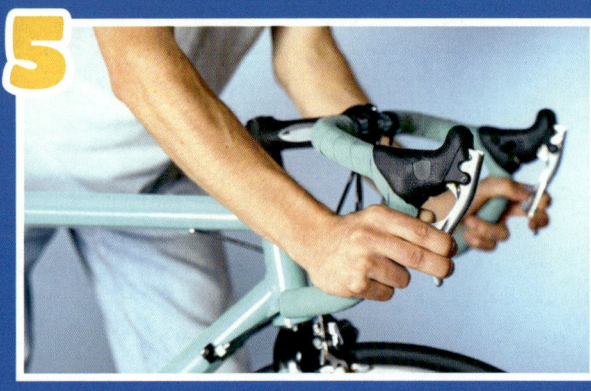

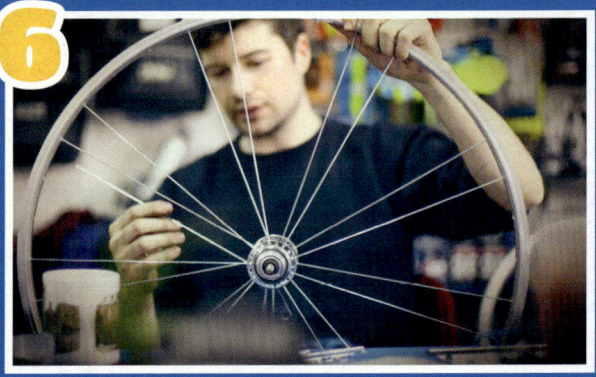

Answers

1.B 2.C 3.A 4.F 5.E 6.D

Key Words

alloy: a combination of two metals

aluminum: a light metal with a silver color

carbon: a nonmetal that is found in coal, diamonds, plants, and animals, and can be mixed with iron to make steel.

electrons: tiny parts of atoms

hub: the center of a wheel

joints: the places where two or more things meet and come together

molds: hollow containers that a material is put into to set shapes

static electricity: builds up on objects and is made when one object rubs against another

tension: the tightness of a rope, wire, or string

titanium: a hard metal that may be found in bicycle frames

welded: when metal is heated at a high temperature to join two parts together

Index

bicycle factory 4, 9, 10, 14, 24
brake levers 23

chain 20, 21, 23

frame 4, 6, 7, 10, 12, 14, 15, 19, 20, 23, 24, 27, 30
frame tubes 7, 9, 10, 11, 12, 30

gears 20, 21, 23, 27
gearshifts 23

handlebar 4, 19, 23

inner tube 18, 19

mining 6, 7

painting 12, 14, 15

rubber tire 4, 17, 18, 19, 22, 28

seat 24, 25
steel factory 9

testing 26, 27, 28

welding 7, 12, 13, 30
wheels 16, 17, 19, 20, 23, 27, 30

Bicycles 31

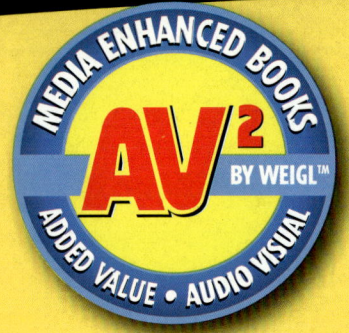

Log on to www.av2books.com

AV² by Weigl brings you media enhanced books that support active learning. Go to www.av2books.com, and enter the special code found on page 2 of this book. You will gain access to enriched and enhanced content that supplements and complements this book. Content includes video, audio, weblinks, quizzes, a slide show, and activities.

AV² Online Navigation

Audio
Listen to sections of the book read aloud.

Book Pages
AV² pages directly correspond to pages in the book.

Video
Watch informative video clips.

Key Words
Study vocabulary, and complete a matching word activity.

Embedded Weblinks
Gain additional information for research.

Try This!
Complete activities and hands-on experiments.

Quizzes
Test your knowledge.

Slide Show
View images and captions, and prepare a presentation.

AV² was built to bridge the gap between print and digital. We encourage you to tell us what you like and what you want to see in the future.

Sign up to be an AV² Ambassador at www.av2books.com/ambassador.

Due to the dynamic nature of the Internet, some of the URLs and activities provided as part of AV² by Weigl may have changed or ceased to exist. AV² by Weigl accepts no responsibility for any such changes. All media enhanced books are regularly monitored to update addresses and sites in a timely manner. Contact AV² by Weigl at 1-866-649-3445 or av2books@weigl.com with any questions, comments, or feedback.